BRAVO!

PLAYALONG
SYMPHONIC
THEMES

The series *for more advanced soloists*

BRAVO! FLUTE

PLAYALONG SYMPHONIC THEMES

AMSCO PUBLICATIONS
part of The Music Sales Group

London / New York / Paris / Sydney / Copenhagen / Berlin / Madrid / Tokyo

Exclusive Distributors:
MUSIC SALES CORPORATION
257 Park Avenue South, New York, NY 10010,
United States of America.

MUSIC SALES LIMITED
Distribution Centre, Newmarket Road,
Bury St Edmunds, Suffolk IP33 3YB,
United Kingdom.

MUSIC SALES PTY LIMITED
20 Resolution Drive, Caringbah, NSW 2229, Australia.

Project management, arranging and recording by Artemis Music Limited.
Cover designed by Michael Bell Design.
Cover photograph courtesy of Alvis Upitis/Getty Images.

Order No. AM994466
ISBN 978-0-8256-3658-5

Printed in the United States of America by
Vicks Lithograph and Printing Corporation

Your Guarantee of Quality:
As publishers, we strive to produce every book to the highest commercial standards.
This book has been carefully designed to minimize awkward page turns and to
make playing from it a real pleasure.
Particular care has been given to specifying acid-free, neutral-sized paper made
from pulps that have not been elemental chlorine bleached.
This pulp is from farmed sustainable forests and
was produced with special regard for the environment.
Throughout, the printing and binding have been planned to ensure a
sturdy, attractive publication, which should give years of enjoyment.
If your copy fails to meet our high standards, please inform us and we will gladly replace it.

www.musicsales.com

"Pastoral" Symphony, 1st Movement

Ludwig van Beethoven

Allegro ma non troppo ♩ = 66

Symphony No. 5, 2nd Movement

Ludwig van Beethoven

Symphony No. 5, 4th Movement

Ludwig van Beethoven

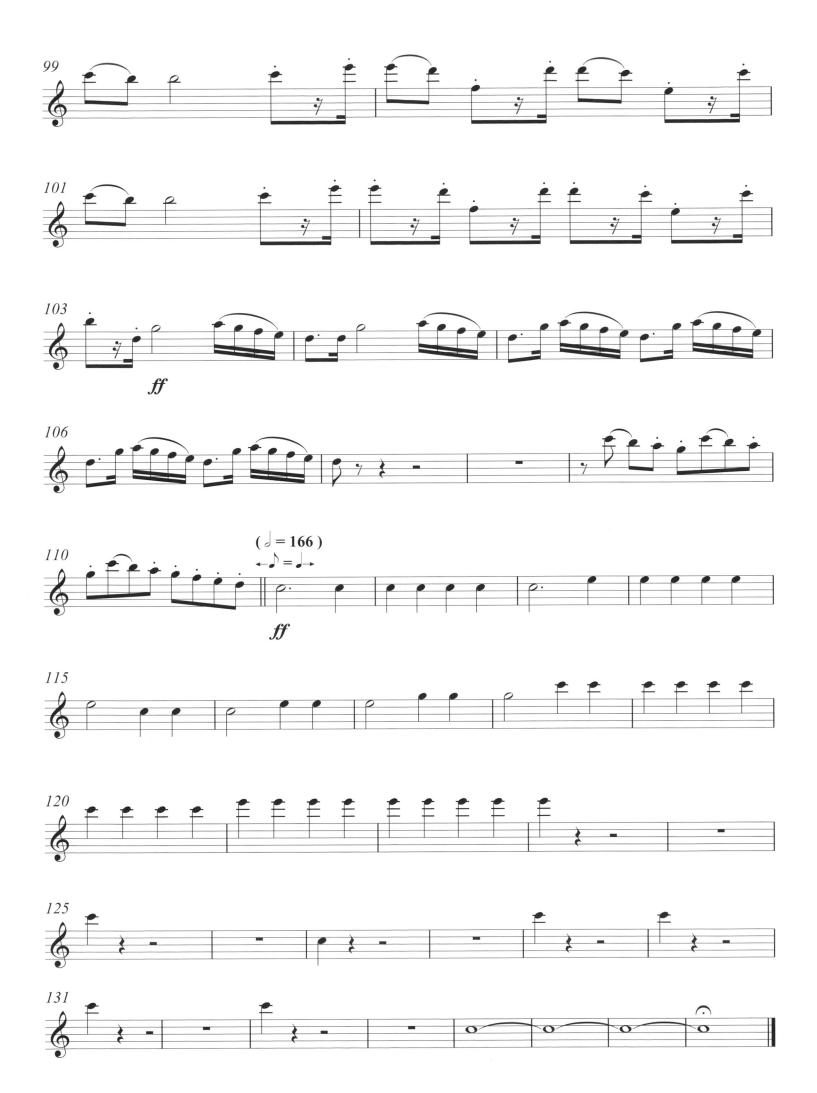

13

Symphony No. 3, 3rd Movement

Poco Allegretto (♪ = 100)

dolce

dim. *dolce*

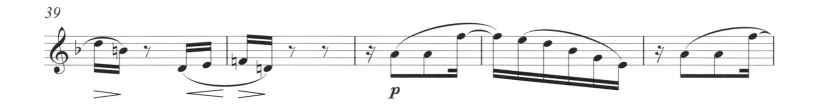

p

p

f

"New World" Symphony, 2nd Movement

Antonin Dvořák

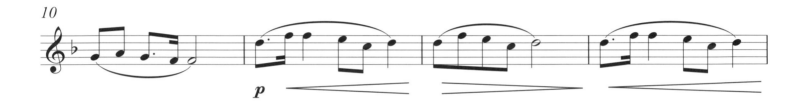

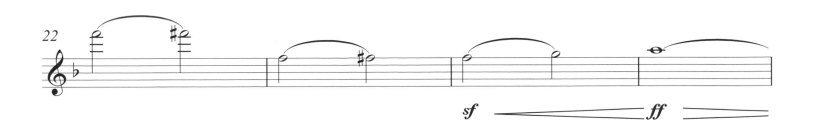

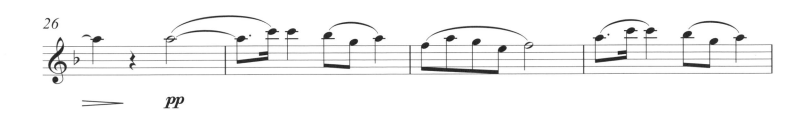

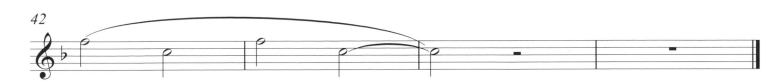

"Surprise" Symphony, 2nd Movement

Joseph Haydn

Andante (♩ = 66)

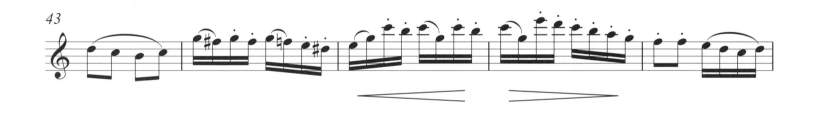

Symphony No. 40, 1st Movement

Wolfgang Amadeus Mozart

Symphony No. 41, 3rd Movement

Allegretto

"Pathétique" Symphony, 1st Movement

Peter Ilyich Tchaikovsky

"Unfinished" Symphony, 1st Movement

Franz Schubert

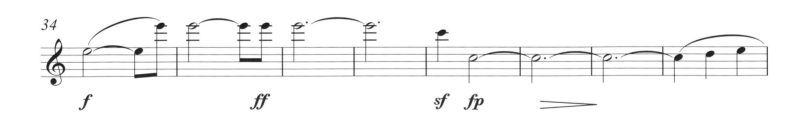

CD TRACK LISTING

Demo tracks followed by backing tracks

TRACKS 1 & 2

"PASTORAL" SYMPHONY

1ST MOVEMENT

LUDWIG VAN BEETHOVEN

TRACKS 3 & 4

SYMPHONY NO. 5

2ND MOVEMENT

LUDWIG VAN BEETHOVEN

TRACKS 5 & 6

SYMPHONY NO. 5

4TH MOVEMENT

LUDWIG VAN BEETHOVEN

TRACKS 7 & 8

SYMPHONY NO. 3

3RD MOVEMENT

JOHANNES BRAHMS

TRACKS 9 & 10

"NEW WORLD" SYMPHONY

2ND MOVEMENT

ANTONÍN DVOŘÁK

TRACKS 11 & 12

"SURPRISE" SYMPHONY

2ND MOVEMENT

JOSEPH HAYDN

TRACKS 13 & 14

SYMPHONY NO. 40

1ST MOVEMENT

WOLFGANG AMADEUS MOZART

TRACKS 15 & 16

SYMPHONY NO. 41

3RD MOVEMENT

WOLFGANG AMADEUS MOZART

TRACKS 17 & 18

"PATHÉTIQUE" SYMPHONY

1ST MOVEMENT

PETER ILYICH TCHAIKOVSKY

TRACKS 19 & 20

"UNFINISHED" SYMPHONY

1ST MOVEMENT

FRANZ SCHUBERT